C000220949

The search for a
better lawn
starts here!

Gardening **organically**

One of the great joys of gardening is to experience the variety of life that a healthy garden contains. A garden managed using organic methods will have far more interest in it than a garden where insecticides and chemicals are used. An organic garden is a more balanced environment, where 'good' creatures such as ladybirds and beetles keep the 'bad' pests and diseases under control.

Organically grown plants also tend to be healthier and stronger than plants that rely on large doses of artificial fertiliser. In healthy soil they grow strong roots and can better withstand attack by pests and diseases. Soil can be kept in top condition by recycling garden waste to make nutritious compost. Growing the right combination of plants in the right place at the right time – by rotating where you plant your veg for example, or choosing shrubs to suit the growing conditions that your garden can offer – can deliver impressive disease-free results.

These are the basic principles of organic growing – use the natural resources you already have to create a balanced and vibrant garden. It's sustainable, cheaper than buying chemicals, easier than you think and great fun. Enjoy your organic gardening.

Whether it's a tiny patch or many acres, few homeowners want to be without a lawn. It is such a versatile feature, providing a visual foil for flower and shrub borders as well as a great spot to relax and a safe place for children to play. But lawns can be troublesome: laying a new one is a daunting prospect, and even well-established lawns get plagued by moss and other weeds. This book shows you how to maintain a great looking lawn using organic methods. The result will be a pleasant area for your family, pets and for wildlife.

Contents

1

What makes a good lawn?

What **makes** a good lawn?

It depends what you want from your lawn! Everyone's an individual, every home is unique. Do you want a fine ornamental lawn? A backdrop to a gorgeous flower border? A children's playground? A hard wearing utility lawn, a wildlife grassy area or even a more delicate but fragrant camomile or herb sward? The choice is always yours.

A good lawn is one which looks great throughout the year, doesn't require constant repair or attention and gives satisfaction to the owner, whether it's used to play on with children and pets or to entertain friends on a summer evening.

Why is a lawn so **important** to a garden?

For hundreds of years the British have been praised for the quality of their lawns. The English lawn is one of the reasons that our country has always been celebrated as a 'green and pleasant land'. In fact our style of lawn has been copied all over the world.

However, just as we take great care to decorate and furnish the rooms in our house, this exceptional room outside requires planning and maintenance, both to ensure luxurious green growth and also to prevent weeds, pests and diseases taking over.

This book shows you:

- how to achieve a great looking lawn in a way that is safe for you, your family, pets and wildlife

- how to diagnose a sick lawn and make it better using only organic methods

- how to keep it looking great.

Renovate or replace?

If your lawn is very old and has not been cared for it will certainly be invaded by weeds, be uneven, washed-out and look tatty. It's easy to diagnose a worn-out lawn. Walk the lawn looking for yellow/light green colours, bare patches and weeds. If the lawn feels very springy then this is a sign of thatch (dead plant remains) which has built up and will encourage moss and disease. Scarifying or raking out will help deal with this problem.

You can renovate a worn out lawn just by following the advice in this book in Chapter 4. However, if you want a truly outstanding lawn it may be best to start again.

***Signs of a sick lawn**
Dog bitch-scorch (top); dry, discoloured and patchy (middle); and (bottom) lawn invaded by weeds and moss.*

Top 10 signs of a sick lawn

1 Discoloured pale green/yellow grass

2 Unevenly cut grass

3 Dead or dried-out grass

4 Uneven surfaces with hollows and bumps

5 Thatch causing a spongy surface

6 More dandylions and daises than grass

7 Bare patches

8 Grass goes brown in dry weather

9 Large areas of moss

10 Turf diseases – like fairy rings and brown patch disease

New lawns **seed** or **turf?**

Seeding is cheaper and a more organic and sustainable approach to creating a lawn - but turf establishes more quickly and may provide a more uniform finish.

Turf quality is generally very good. Obviously you have to check that the turf contains the correct grass types for your needs and is from a reputable supplier. Also inspect the turves on delivery for weeds. Invariably chemical fertilisers and weed killers will have been used in growing the turf but they do not linger in the soil and should not affect your garden in the longer term. If in doubt ask the supplier exactly how the turf is treated.

Seeding is the organic - and cheaper - option. A good tip is to order your seed mixture early in the year so that you get good quality seed and can sow when the conditions are right. Typical sowing rates are 35-70g/m^2 which must be evenly spread over the surface – so measure your lawn area carefully before ordering. Always order a bit more than required then you can use the same type of seed for running repairs. If you want an alternative lawn such as camomile, then you must either grow from seed or alternatively, for a non-flowering camomile lawn, '*Treneague*' is available as plants.

Choose the **lawn that is right** for you

There are thousands of different grasses to choose from but only a few that can withstand the regular cutting needed to produce a lush dense green lawn. But remember that an organic lawn that is not dosed with artificial fertilisers will need less cutting. Usually lawn seed is purchased as a blend of rye, fescue and bent grasses to form the ideal home lawn.

The **ornamental lawn** comes from fine leaved grasses such as bents and fescues growing in a dense carpet style. With a gorgeous light green and soft texture many people like the luxurious elegance one of these lawns adds to their home. Beautiful to look at they may be, but they don't like heavy use. If you have a sandy soil this lawn will grow well but you may need to water it regularly in the summer.

The **utility lawn** is perfect to take the rough and tumble of a growing family and pets. These are

From springy moss and weed filled patch to a level green sward – assess your lawn and then renovate or replace.

made from mixtures containing hard-wearing rye grass and the more elegant fescues. Rye grass has a thicker leaf blade and is much faster growing so damage is more quickly repaired. If you have a heavier soil these grasses will produce a rich dark green carpet that looks great all year round and is able to cope with hot dry summers.

Camomile or herb lawns don't require much mowing and might be an attractive option for a small sunny area of lawn - but they can't survive regular use. Alternatively, if you have made room for a **wildlife area** in the garden, you might think about a **wildflower lawn** (see page 39). Here you can tolerate more of those 'weeds' and relax your mowing regime, cutting just a few times a year. Traditional hay meadows are cut just once (in August), but flowers are best encouraged by cutting in June and September, with a hand-shear trim occasionally if it gets too untidy. Don't add any fertiliser as wildflowers actually do best in soils with low nutrients. Clear away the cuttings to the compost heap. As well as looking pretty the longer grass, punctuated by flowers, offers shelter to insects and other small creatures.

The **organic** approach

Why **avoid** chemicals?

The modern approach to getting good quality lawns has been to use chemical aids. This might be as a seed dressing, fertiliser coating or control for pests and diseases. In most cases this involves using man-made synthetic chemicals. It is thought that these chemicals may have a damaging long-term effect on our environment. Certainly chemical residues are appearing in water supplies and the food chain and these seem to be affecting our ecology. Of course dosing your lawn regularly with chemicals is not just an expensive business - it can suppress the natural life in the soil and kill the food that birds and insects depend upon.

We believe a better approach is to work with nature to produce a vibrant lawn. It is possible to create and maintain a beautiful lawn by using organic principles. With the help of modern tools it need not even be hard work!

In this book we show you how to achieve a great lawn through regular mowing, composting, raking, scarification, aeration, spiking, top dressing, manual weeding and working with worms. And don't worry, if you're not familiar with these terms they will be explained as we go along.

Lawn care – the basics

In organic gardening, prevention is always better than cure. Applying weed killers or artificial fertilisers will only mask the symptoms for a short while - the cause of the problems will still be there. So regular maintenance is the answer. Two of the key activities for keeping your lawn in good order are: making holes in the lawn with a fork to let air in and raking out thatch (dead grass and weeds) to allow the grass to prosper. If the grass is truly healthy the weeds won't get a look in!

ORGANIC FEEDING:

Whilst remembering that if the conditions are kept right you will not need to feed the lawn very much, there are advantages to applying compost as a top dressing and perhaps a foliar feed of seaweed extract to help 'green' your lawn. Garden compost is suitable for top dressing your lawn – see *Create Compost* in the *Green Essentials* series for more infomation.

As with many aspects of organic gardening, the key to success is in the soil. If the soil below the grass is in poor condition or compacted by use, the grass will suffer.

Similarly if the grass is denied air, sunlight or water because of either competing plants, trees, weeds or fallen leaves, then the grass will not grow healthily. And the healthier the grass and its roots are, the less likely it is that lawn diseases or pests will begin to take over.

Here's a **typical maintenance schedule** to keep your lawn in good condition:

- Autumn and spring are the two key times for maintenance.

- Remove thatch (the dead grass and material under the grass) by raking or scarifying with a mower attachment or dedicated machine.

- Aerate the soil by spiking the lawn all over with an ordinary or hollow-tined fork. Compaction and lack of air in the soil can be a major cause of lawn problems.

- After performing these two tasks, spread a thin dressing of bulky organic material over the grass – this should be a mix of leafmould, soil / compost and sand; it is a good idea to work this into the soil using a brush or rake. The ratio of leafmould, soil and sand will vary according to the nature of the soil in your garden.

- In spring you could follow these procedures by spreading some additional (organic) lawn seed over the grass to ensure lush, dense growth.

LAWN DON'TS

- Try to avoid walking on grass when it is excessively wet, frosty or there is snow on the ground.

- Do not cut your grass too short – this will allow weeds to flourish and weaken the grass.

- Avoid excessive shade and drought – for example where a nearby tree takes both moisture and light, you might be better re-siting that piece of lawn.

action stations

1 **Choose** the right lawn for your home. Will it be ornamental, utility, wildlife or camomile? Check if your soil is sandy or clay.

2 **Renovate or replace?** Depending upon the condition of your lawn decide whether to renovate the existing lawn or replace with new.

3 **Decide** on turf or seed. As a rule of thumb, turf is quicker but seed is cheaper and more sustainable.

4 **Order** turf and seed early in the year and avoid problems from late supplies.

2

Know your lawn

Know **your lawn**

Grass is an excellent plant for gardens. It grows all year round even at low temperatures and will therefore stand regular cutting.

Through understanding nature's cycles of growth, we can manage the lawn to always be in the best condition.

Lawn grasses work in harmony with the soil and atmosphere to produce lush growth. Grass spreads by horizontally spreading stems called rhizomes (underground) and stolons (overground). We can manage the lawn to encourage this growth and ensure an increasingly dense carpet of leaf blades. However grass is a very shallow fibrous rooting plant and easily suffers from drought in hot weather.

From the soil, grass takes many nutrients including nitrogen (N) for growing, phosphorus (P) for roots, potassium (K) for disease resistance and cell strength and magnesium (Mg) to help turn sunlight into sugar (photosynthesis). Plenty of air is needed in the soil to encourage growth and prevent disease. That's why we need to aerate the soil regularly and keep off the lawn in wet weather to avoid compaction.

Mowing

How you cut your lawn will have a major impact on how it looks. Mowing will help to weaken and kill off weeds. However, the more vigorous weeds may take 2-3 years to die until all the stored energy in their roots has been exhausted from the constant pressure of mowing their leaves off.

Cutting too short will also weaken the grass. First decide on how short you want your grass. Then set your mower blades to the right height to maintain the appearance you want.

On an **ornamental lawn** this should be around 5-10mm and on a utility lawn 25-50mm tall. The finer the grass, the closer the mow. Mow regularly and don't allow the grass to grow more than twice the desired height before cutting. But beware of consistently cutting your lawn too short – you might scalp the turf and encourage weeds. If you've left the grass too long bring it back down to the required length over several cuts.

Before mowing it's a good idea to use a stiff yard brush to remove debris and brush the worm casts (small piles of earth on the surface of the lawn) into the soil. Brushing also raises the grass up to meet the mower blade. While you're doing this make a mental note of any unevenness or weeds you want to deal with.

In spring and autumn, and in very dry weather, leave the grass a little longer.

Cylinder or rotary mower? Cylinder (manual or powered) for stripes and ornamental lawns, rotary for utility lawns and speed.

Mulching mowers or mulching attachments for your ordinary mower will chop the grass cuttings again into fine pieces that rot down quickly providing extra nutrients.

The next question is **which lawn mower?** You have two choices either a **rotary or cylinder** mower. You could use a cylinder push-mower (still available) and get fit as you mow! Or the choice is electric or petrol powered. If you want neat stripes down the turf you simply have to have a cylinder mower and cut each strip in opposite directions. They produce a fine even cut suited to ornamental lawns. Mow regularly to 5-12mm in the summer - though an organic lawn where artificial fertilisers are not being used, will grow more slowly. Increase the height of cut in the autumn and winter to 15-20mm. If you have a utility or camomile lawn and are not bothered about stripes, then a rotary mower will give excellent results. They are also ideal for cutting down long or rough grass and for use on uneven surfaces.

Grass is about 95% water, after a few weeks on the compost heap it will shrink to less than a quarter of its original volume. However, it decomposes slowly; add some leaves or other woody material to help speed up the process.

Clippings

A lawn can produce a lot of clippings – you can cut 1 tonne from 1000 square metres of grass in a year! In the spring and autumn, or if you have left the lawn a little too long, collect them after cutting. In the main growing season, clippings can be left on a regularly mown lawn without causing any problems. They will soon decay into the lawn, feeding the grass with exactly what it needs.

A relatively new invention is the 'mulching mower'. This cuts, and recuts, the mowings into tiny pieces, then pushes them out of sight, deep into the lawn, avoiding the problem of clumps of grass that can be tramped back into the house. Never having to collect up the mowings, or stop to empty the grass box, can cut mowing time by half. If you do collect up the mowings, don't waste their goodness. Mix them up in your compost heap, or with autumn leaves in plastic bags so they will rot more quickly, or use them as a mulch around shrubs and established vegetable plants. If you still have too many mowings, consider reducing the area of your lawn or mow it less often!

Weeds

A weed is simply any plant growing in the wrong place. Typical lawn weeds include: annual meadow grass, dandelion, daisies, plantains, buttercup, white clover, yarrow and moss.

Weeds are easy to spot. Walk the lawn and if you see something that isn't grass then it's a weed. The low growing weeds survive because they are untouched by the mower. They are easily spotted by their rosette-patterned leaves hugging the soil.

For the most part, weeds are kept under control by regular mowing, aeration and scarification. If you leave it too long between cuts other weeds such as groundsel, couch grass and thistles may also invade. Even a quick rake before mowing will help towards keeping weeds at bay.

Weeding: A good way for your children to earn some pocket money! Extract weeds with a small trowel or knife ensuring that all of the root is removed.

The most environmentally friendly way to remove weeds is to dig them up with a small trowel or knife making certain that all the root is removed.

Some weeds, like clover, are beneficial in lawns as they fix nitrogen from the atmosphere and can stimulate healthy green grass growth. However, clover left completely unchecked can take over. Altering the height of mower cut (and feeding the grass if necessary) will enable you to achieve the desired grass/clover balance on a utility lawn. For an ornamental lawn you should apply a more strict mowing and raking regime.

  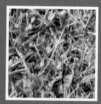 

 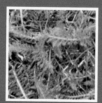

Weeds (from top left): Dandelion seed, dandelion in flower, clover, annual meadow grass, buttercup and yarrow. Depending upon the kind of lawn you want, you can banish weeds completely or, if you prefer, tolerate a little diversity.

Common **lawn weeds** and how to deal with them **organically**

Controlling weeds organically is about constant vigilance and physically removing them. Weeds are only plants growing in the wrong place so when you remove them, put them in the compost and re-use their valuable nutrients. Perennial weeds will need a 'hot' compost heap to kill the seeds.

Weeds not only affect the appearance of your lawn but can also take essential nutrients from the soil and cause the lawn to deteriorate further. If left uncontrolled, weeds such as daisies and clover quickly develop into clumps, effectively shading out the grass completely. They need to be kept firmly under control with regular raking out and removal.

The annual **weed campaign**

By mid to end of April various weeds, such as creeping buttercup, dandelion and plantains, will start to threaten the lawn. The exception is black medick, which tends to appear late May. As with all garden weeds, it is advisable to control them early - before they become a serious nuisance and return more seed to the ground. The soil usually has a bank of weed seeds in it, so prepare for an annual campaign.

The main culprits:

Moss. Moss is a real sign of a lawn problem particularly in shady areas and where fertility is low. The main reason for moss is surface compaction, with the moss thriving on the layer of moisture unable to drain away on the surface of the lawn. The keys to avoiding a moss invasion on the lawn are good aeration, drainage and soil fertility plus avoiding scalping the lawn when mowing.

Daisy. The daisy is particularly common in closely-mown turf. Having some daisies can look pleasant but if they get out of control they can start strangling the grass.

Great Plantain. Plantains, such as greater plantain produce rosettes of leathery and prominently-ribbed leaves. Plantains tend to flower May - September.

Self heal. A hairy creeping weed, rooting at nodes. Oval leaves grow in pairs. Purple flowers appear from June onwards. Most common in wet heavy soils.

Ribwort. A common perennial weed with narrow, ribbed leaves, cylindrical brown flower heads borne on long stalks from May to September.

Yarrow. A creeping perennial weed producing fine dark green leaves (similar to carrot tops). If allowed to flower, clusters of white flowers from mid-summer onwards. Found on all soil types.

White clover. White flowered, creeping perennial weed with stems that root at nodes. Three leaflets, each with a central mark, are borne on a long stalk. Favours heavy soils and is relatively easy to control.

Ribwort

Great Plantain

Daisy

White Clover

Some weeds will look nice to some people – beauty is in the eye of the beholder. A lawn with many daisies for example can be especially pleasing.

Lawn **pests** and **diseases**

Pests

Leatherjackets. Leatherjackets (pictured), are the grubs of the crane fly commonly known as the daddy long legs. Crane flies lay their eggs in the lawn in late summer with the grubs (larvae) hatching in the autumn. It is the grubs that cause the damage, feeding on the roots and stem bases resulting in patches of yellow or brown grass. Minimise the impact of crane fly lavae by reducing damp conditions and keeping the lawn well aerated - leave the rest to the birds.

Moles. Moles are another difficult lawn problem – they're attracted by plenty of worms in the soils but unless you're prepared to get the professionals in to trap them, you may have to live with them.

Diseases

Fusarium patch (Snow mould). A common fungal disease prevalent in autumn and in spring after long lying snow. Symptoms are areas of yellowing grass eventually merging to extensive brown areas. **Avoid nitrogen rich fertiliser and spike (aerate) regularly.**

Red thread (Corticium disease). Pinkish red and bleached areas of grass. Grass with insufficient nutrients is prone to attack. **Feed with organic fertiliser in spring and summer and spike regularly.**

Working with **worms**

At first glance earthworms may be a nuisance to a lawn because of the unsightly worm casts left on the surface. However, in reality they are vital because they create aeration and drainage channels in the soil helping to maintain a healthy lawn.

Earthworms also help to:

- Reduce fertiliser use because casts are rich in nutrients
- Mix dead and decaying plant remains
- Rotavate the soil
- Stimulate root growth
- Increase availability of plant nutrients
- Recycle nutrients and break down decaying plant matter
- Supply food for some ground feeding birds such as blackbird, robin and thrush

That's why we welcome worms in the lawn. The casts can easily be brushed in leaving a beautiful lawn behind. If you find any worms on the surface, pick them up and put them straight onto the compost heap where they will love munching through old plant remains.

action stations

1 **Choose your mower.** Cylinder for stripes or rotary for speed. Use a push cylinder mower for fitness and environmental care!

2 **Compost your clippings.** A year's worth of mowings will return significant quantity of nitrogen to the lawn and other nutrients too.

3 **Weeds.** Dig up and remove using a trowel or knife.

4 **Mulch.** Use a mulching mower to chop cuttings finely to feed the soil.

5 **For more information about compost** see *Create Compost* in the *Green Essentials* series.

Creating your perfect lawn

Creating your perfect lawn from scratch

Everyone wants a perfect lawn. But the key to success is preparation. Get all the tools and equipment you need together before you start and take the time to prepare a flat surface on which to lay turf or sow seed.

Prepare the **soil**

1   Remove and dispose of all the existing turf (grass and its base of soil and roots) or plant material by cutting with a spade and placing in the compost heap.

2   Go over the soil and remove all the unwanted large stones, bits of wood or other material that will hinder a perfectly flat surface.

3   If your soil is very compacted this is also the time to rotavate or dig it over to create a well drained and aerated lawn.

Preparation, preparation, preparation – the key to success. Top: Cleared and rotavated. Above: Hard raking to create a level surface.

4 Apply leafmould (well-rotted leaves) or your own garden compost to the soil – particularly if you have taken off the old turf. This will provide a base that is both nutritious and a good consistency.

5 Rake the soil hard into a level surface. Break up the large lumps as you go. If your soil is very uneven you will need to buy some top soil to spread into the hollows and then rake. Keep raking level. After a while your eye will be fine-tuned to the ground and you will easily see any hollows that need filling or peaks that need levelling. If you prefer, you can use a long spirit level to check your accuracy.

6 Shuffle over the soil, firming it with your heel so that the lawn won't sink when you walk on it. When you're satisfied with the surface you are ready to sow seed or lay turf.

Adding top soil to an uneven and troublesome surface (top). Shuffle over the soil (above) to prevent your lawn from sinking.

Turf laying

The best time to lay turf is autumn or early spring allowing the roots to grow firmly into the soil. The golden rule of laying turf is 'never walk on it'. Avoid this by using boards to spread your weight. Make certain you use a reputable supplier for a quality turf. Don't buy meadow grass from the local farm! It will be peppered with weeds.

1 Just before you start laying, rake the patch where the turf is going down again to ensure it is level.

2 Unroll the turf and start laying it along one edge, working backwards from this point. You can move the turf around on the soil using a fork and make sure that the edges butt-up together tightly. When you lay the next row start in a different place so that all the joins are not in the same place – as you would if you were laying a wood floor.

3   Use a sharp knife or half-moon iron to cut the edges or trim the turf to the shape you want. To get an immediate striped effect simply lay each row in opposite directions. When your lawn is well rooted the stripes can be maintained by mowing each strip in opposite directions.

4   Firm the newly laid turf so that the roots are in close contact with the soil. Lay out walking boards and walk over the entire lawn, moving the boards around to make certain that every inch of turf is covered.

5   Use a hose with a fine rose and thoroughly water the new turf so that it gets off to a good start. If the weather is hot you will have to keep watering every few days until the grass is established – this will take 2-3 weeks.

6   Give the turf a good chance to get established. Keep off the grass (for at least 10 days) until you are certain it has properly rooted into the soil and won't move when you step on it.

To get an immediate striped effect, lay your rows of turf in opposite directions. Walk the plank to ensure that newly laid turf is firmed and that the roots are in contact with the soil.

After all the hard work pour yourself a cool drink, grab a chair and then sit back and enjoy!

Creating a **wildflower lawn**

Not everybody wants a neat, meticulously clipped lawn; many of us prefer something a little wilder that provides food and shelter for insects. A wildflower meadow can be a striking and impressive alternative.

It is the diversity of species of grass and flower that make a meadow so attractive. The key to this diversity is low soil fertility. Where soil is poor, especially low in phosphate, coarse vigorous grasses and weeds do not have their normal competitive edge, so giving fine grasses and flowers a chance to thrive. Select a wildflower and grass seed mix to suit your soil type (making sure that the wildflower seed is from native British stock). Sow in autumn for a June flowering or in early spring for a later flowering. Allow the wildflowers to set seed before cutting back and removing 'hay'. Then each autumn or spring the earth should be forked over or rotavated to stimulate germination of the fallen seed. When you do mow this kind of lawn, keep the blades at least 12mm higher than usual, remove all clippings and do not use fertilisers or weedkillers.

If you've got a poor lawn anyway, why not try leaving it to see what you get – or help it along by clearing moss and sowing a mix of lawn seed and wildflowers.

Seed sowing

Sowing seed is easy and many people prefer it to turf laying. It is also a much more sustainable and organic option. But care is needed to ensure even sowing. Seeding is also used to repair bare patches. The best times of year to sow are spring and early autumn, although grass will germinate throughout the year, especially if the weather is mild. After 10 days the seeds will have germinated and the leaf blades will be showing. On weedy ground it is a good idea to leave the prepared soil bare for a week or two to allow a flush of weed seedlings to appear. These can be lightly hoed off before sowing the grass seed.

1   Most grasses are sown at about $35g/m^2$, but check the packet and follow the supplier's instructions. Sowing is completed in two passes. Half is sown in one direction then the second half at right angles to the

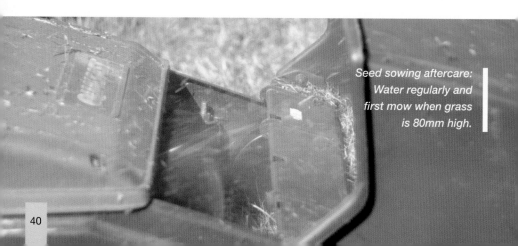

Seed sowing aftercare: Water regularly and first mow when grass is 80mm high.

first. Another technique is to mix the seed with some topsoil or sand which is then raked evenly over the whole lawn area.

2   If you are sowing by hand, mark out the soil into $1m^2$ blocks using string - this will help you to sow the area evenly. If you have a large garden to sow, hire a seed drill calibrated for grass. It will save time and give you a very even finish.

3   Either use a roller on the seed bed or walk over it on boards to firm the seed into the soil.

4   Water the seed bed with a fine spray to encourage germination. Keep watering every few days so that it doesn't dry out.

5   Stop birds eating your seed and dust-bathing. Try tightly stretched black netting or string tied with lengths of silver foil, raised above the bed. This usually deters birds quite well.

Aftercare (seed sown lawn)

1   Water regularly making sure that the seed or turf does not dry out.
    Do not walk on the new surface until you are sure it has properly rooted.

2   First mow when grass is 80mm high, gradually reducing the height of the cut over the season, down to your preferred height.

action stations

1 **Preparation.** Spend time clearing, digging and rotavating the surface. Rake over the soil until it's totally flat; add topsoil to troublesome uneven surfaces. Check on the organic status of the top soil or soil improvers that you buy.

2 **Turf.** Lay turf in rows going in opposite directions to achieve an immediate striped effect. Use boards to walk on it. Use a sharp knife or edging iron to cut the edges.

3 **Sowing (the organic option).** Sow evenly at about 35g/m². Use netting or string to stop birds eating your seed.

4 **Aftercare.**
Water new lawns thoroughly, especially in hot weather.
Turf. Keep off new turf for at least 10 days or until you're certain it has established properly. Allow 2-3 weeks for turf to become established.
Seeded lawn. First mow when grass is 80mm high.

Improving and
maintaining

Methods and tools for improving and maintaining an existing lawn

As your lawn gets older one of the biggest problems will be weeds invading the grass. Some people tolerate a level of weeds - but left to run riot they will take over from the grass. Get into the habit now of inspecting your lawn for colour, weeds, thatch, moss and worn out patches that might need replacing or re-seeding. We will show you how to improve and maintain a first rate lawn through good lawnsmanship.

Aeration

A major part of good lawn management is to get air into the soil so that the roots can flourish and also to create drainage channels to help drain excess water. Lawns suffer from heavy pedestrian traffic causing compaction. Aeration helps to correct this and maintain your lawn in top condition.

Forking is the simplest form of aeration. Just walk over the lawn stabbing the ground with your garden fork. Make sure it goes in at least 100mm. Keep walking as you do this creating some heave as you bend the fork in the soil – hard work but well worthwhile.

Solid-tining produces a more even pattern of aeration channels. It's very easy to do. Just keep rolling the wheeled aerator all over the lawn. These machines are also excellent at breaking up a thatch layer.

Hollow-tining (using a wheeled aerator which you can hire or buy) provides a More complex aeration technique. A core of soil is removed creating a much larger and more stable channel. This makes it ideal for lawns on clay or waterlogged soils. Waste soil cores are swept up afterwards and deposited on the compost heap.

Aeration: Forking (top) is the simplest form of aeration, but can be hard work. Solid-tining (middle) produces an even pattern of aeration channels whilst hollow-tining removes a core of soil and is ideal on waterlogged soils. (You can usually hire machines for both solid and hollow-tining).

Top dressing

After aeration treatments it's a good idea to apply a top dressing mixture of fine garden compost/soil/sand to help improve to fill hollows and encourage dense grass growth. It should be spread on the soil and raked in evenly. This helps to maintain an even surface and also fills the cavities caused by frost, roots and worms creating excellent drainage and aeration channels. It is especially important for the fine grasses of an ornamental lawn. After you've finished raking and brushing no top dressing should be left visible on the grass surface.

Materials for top dressing
Sand - medium grade, lime free
Soil - use good garden soil, fine garden compost or even used potting compost
Peat-substitute - use leafmould, fine grade bark or greenwaste compost.
(Reduce the proportion of sand on light soils).

After aeration and scarifying, apply a top dressing (at a ratio of 1:3:6 organic matter/soil/sand) to fill hollows and encourage growth.

Feeding the lawn

Regular feeding may be needed for a very high quality lawn, but a general purpose sward should only be fed as required. If it is a good colour and growing well feeding only encourages more growth and more mowing! Poor growth and yellowing indicates action is required – though check that compaction is not the problem. Recycling mowings is the easiest way to keep the grass fed. A year's worth of mowings can return over 1kg of nitrogen per 100sq metres of lawn, and lots of other nutrients too. Clover is a vital plant in organic growing and in a lawn adds nitrogen that it takes up from the air; some seed mixes now include clover.

Organic fertilisers

Organic lawn feeds are made from recycled plant and animal materials, and minerals. They decay slowly to feed the grass over a period of time. Artificial fertilisers may provide a quick hit but they do not provide lasting benefit.

Spring feed

Nitrogen feeds to give the grass a boost

- Sieved garden compost
- Blood, fish and bone meal
- Branded (certified organic) lawn feed
- Seaweed meal

Liquid seaweed watered on direct will green up a lawn.

Autumn feed

Low nitrogen to avoid encouraging leafy growth but to keep the grass in good health over winter.

- Branded (certified organic) autumn lawn feed
- Green waste compost

Liming

Grass does not thrive on acid soils (pH below 5.5). Symptoms of acidity include thin grass, weeds such as moss, woodrush and sheep's sorrel, and few worms - loose sandy soils are often acidic. Adding lime will make the soil more alkaline.

Remember to look for indications that an 'organic' product has either come from a **certified organic source** or has been certified as suitable for use in an organic system.

Look for the HDRA or Soil Association logos on products that claim to be organic.

Through the **seasons**

Winter

Even in winter there is work to do. Remember that in frost, snow or very wet weather leave the turf well alone or you will cause damage to the grass and compact the soil.

The key activity is to aerate the soil, both to allow water to escape from the surface and also to enable air to circulate and stimulate root growth in the spring. You can either hire a machine or walk the lawn spiking with a garden fork.

Keep weeding and scarifying (hard raking) regularly throughout the winter until you are certain that all the thatch (dead plant remains) has been removed.

49

Spring

Your lawn should be disease-free and healthy following the winter maintenance schedule. In spring the grass is ready to explode into new growth. Start mowing regularly taking off the clippings to compost until the weather warms up. Tidy up lawn edges. Top dress with fine garden compost/sand/leafmould if required. Dig up and remove any weeds. Re-seed bare patches and lay any new turf. Spring is also the best time to sow camomile seeds.

Summer

The lawn will be growing vigorously. Keep cutting the grass at the correct height for your use. This could be as low as 5-10mm on an ornamental lawn to 50mm on a utility lawn used by children and pets. In drought conditions

Spring is the time to dig up and remove any weeds, re-seed bare patches, lay any new turf and to start mowing again.

Get your mower blades sharpened annually and regularly remove built up debris.

raise the height of cut. Mowing is easily the most important task to affect the quality of your lawn. Scarify to remove moss and weeds. Camomile lawns only need a light trim with shears to keep them neat and tidy. Keep weeding. If it is very dry you may also need to water the lawn every few days, though once established most lawns will survive without watering even if the grass goes brown in the summer.

Autumn is the time to scarify (hard rake) the lawn to reduce moss and remove dead and decaying plant material.

Autumn

Keep cutting the lawn if necessary. As with all organic growing the focus at this time of year should be on preventing disease by making sure the plant has the right conditions. Strengthen the grass prior to wet autumn and winter weather with a fertiliser containing just phosphorus and potassium for slow steady growth.

Autumn is also the time to scarify (hard rake) the lawn to remove all the dead and decaying plant material. Keep weeding by hand to remove any undesirable plants. Sow any bare patches and lay new turf. Raise the height of cut as winter approaches. Complete your aeration programme. Repair bumps and hollows with top soil. If the hollow is more than 25mm deep then cut the turf open and insert new top soil under the turf making sure that it is level. Rake up autumn leaves, or run the mower over them to chop them up. They will soon disappear into the soil and improve its structure.

Perfect lawn - top tips

- **Choose** a lawn that is right for you – ornamental, utility, wildlife or even a camomile or herb
- **Preparation** of the soil is the key to success. Rake soil into an even surface, add fine garden compost and/or soil improvers (certified organic)
- Use **high quality** turf or seed
- **Brush** your lawn before mowing
- **Mow** regularly – but don't cut the grass too short
- **Scarify** in spring and autumn to remove old grass and weeds
- **Aerate** the soil using a fork or tiner
- **Remove** all weeds using a trowel or knife
- **Trim** the edges for a perfect finish
- **Use** a mulching mower

Owning and managing a lawn is something everyone can enjoy. It is a rewarding experience to see how your work pays off. If you follow the advice given in this book you should get an attractive lawn and hours of enjoyment for yourself and your family. Look forward to those hot summer days stretched out on the lawn in your chair or enjoying a family barbecue.

– Good luck and happy gardening!

Want more organic gardening help?

Then join HDRA, the national charity
for organic gardening, farming and food.

As a member of HDRA you'll gain-
- free access to our Gardening Advisory Service
- access to our three gardens in Warwickshire, Kent and Essex and to 10 more gardens around the UK
- opportunities to attend courses and talks or visit other gardens on Organic Gardens Open Weekends
- discounts when ordering from the Organic Gardening Catalogue
- discounted membership of the Heritage Seed Library
- quarterly magazines full of useful information

You'll also be supporting-
- the conservation of heritage seeds
- an overseas organic advisory service to help small-scale farmers in the tropics
- Duchy Originals HDRA Organic Gardens for Schools
- HDRA Organic Food For All campaign
- research into organic agriculture

To join HDRA ring: 024 7630 3517
email: enquiries@hdra.org.uk
or visit our website: www.hdra.org.uk
Charity No. 298104

Resources

HDRA the organic organisation
www.hdra.org.uk
024 7630 3517

Soil Association the heart of
organic food and farming
www.soilassociation.org
0117 929 0661

MAIL ORDER

The Organic Gardening Catalogue

Organic seeds, composts, raised
beds, barriers, traps and other
organic gardening sundries. All
purchases help to fund the HDRA's
charity work.
www.organiccatalogue.com
0845 1301304

Green Gardener Lawn fertiliser
www.greengardener.co.uk
01394 420087

Rooster – Greenvale Farms Ltd

Organic fertiliser
www.rooster.uk.com
01677 422953

Tamar Organics

www.tamarorganics.co.uk
01822 834887

The Wormcast Company

Organic fertiliser
www.thewormcastcompany.com
0845 605 5000

who, what, where, when and why organic?

for all the answers and tempting offers go to www.whyorganic.org

- Mouthwatering offers on organic produce
- Organic places to shop and stay across the UK
- Seasonal recipes from celebrity chefs
- Expert advice on your food and health
- Soil Association food club – join for just £1 a month

Soil Association
the heart of organic food & farming